Rock Your Soul

The Down-to-Earth Guide
to Mastering Your Mind

NICHOLE EATON

For Camryn and Kylie, my tiny muses, may your futures be a combination of pushing my buttons and shattering glass ceilings. You are both unstoppable, gregarious, and this book wouldn't exist without you. Love you to the moon and back.

P.S. Girls can do anything.

CONTENTS

INTRODUCTION

I Didn't See You There

> *"It all begins and ends in your mind.*
> *What you give power to*
> *has power over you, if you allow it."*
> —*Leon Brown*

I was asked to write a book. I'm kidding, I wasn't, but I thought it would sound way cooler if I had someone approach me, like, "Hey Nichole, we'd love it if you wrote this book." I guess in some ways I have been asked, just not by anything human. There's always been a certainty in my heart that I was born to write. So, if you hate this book, don't tell me.

Anyway, welcome! Glad you could make it. I'd shake your hand but you're there and I'm here, and, well, my palms are sweatier than rap star, Eminem. Did

1

you know that nervousness and excitement have nearly identical physiological feelings? So, I will take that sweaty palms, heart-racing sensation that some might call raging anxiety and label it excitement. Excitement feels better than anxiety. Woohoo! *Brainpower!*

I can barely contain my excitement in sharing all of this juicy, delicious information with you. I truly believe the information tucked between these pages has the capacity to change your life and the way you look at the world. But before we start, there are a few things you should know about me: I have an obsession with the human condition and a total fascination with how the brain works. I truly believe your thoughts are the most powerful agent for change. Lastly, I love to bake made-from-scratch cupcakes. *Okay, so the last one is a little irrelevant... but you wouldn't say that if you tasted my bourbon chocolate cupcakes with salted caramel frosting.*

As a Mental Health Counselor and Life Coach for the last 10+ years, I have had the absolute pleasure of working with people from all walks of life. Clients gifted me the experience of holding their hand while facing some real gruesome shit. I've always felt honored by complete strangers trusting me to join their journey. Life can be effing scary. We can face some very real fears, as well as fears we only imagine in our heads. The good news? Most of our worries, doubts, lack of boundaries, and other junk keeping us from living a happier, healthier life are exactly that—made up!

Life primarily exists in our perception in our mind. Can you imagine how messy that territory gets after years and years of storing thousands of experiences? The memory of when your first boyfriend broke up with you is stored right next to the time you had a few too many margaritas celebrating your acceptance into grad school. All of those mixed feelings, relationships, and experiences are jumbled up in your memory bank.

Perhaps you're wondering, "How do we keep it all straight?" The truth? We don't! Researchers have

found there is no particular accuracy in our thoughts or interpretations of the meaning of events.[1] Envision a time when you waved back to someone who was actually not waving to you, but to the person behind you. Our memories are not necessarily real or fact-based, either. We skew and mold memories and experiences to fit our beliefs and perceptions about the world. *Mind blown!* I like to think that I have a great grip on the way my mind works, but sometimes my brain still ventures off into curious spaces. *Like when I end up lying in bed at night recalling that time my sixth-grade boyfriend dumped me, after telling me I had a mustache. Screw you, Josh!*

What I hope you realize is your little inaccurate brain is wicked powerful and manhandling how you experience your life. This book will give you both understanding and tools to put some reins on the wild horse that is your head. All the knowledge between these pages will help you trade out the fear-based bologna that you've been repeating for years on end for an upgraded model—spam, perhaps? *What is an upgrade from bologna? Anyone?* Because the truth is, as easily as we can create a scary, dark perceptual world that makes you want to dig a ditch and stay there, we can instead choose to create a way of thinking about the world that makes you feel all unicorns and rainbows. *Or at least happier, if unicorns and rainbows aren't your jam.*

Choosing better thoughts and a new perception, intentionally facing fears and redirecting your focus back to your hopes and dreams, is the magical recipe for creating a life to be geeked about. And who doesn't want to be geeked? *Do people still say geeked? Did anyone ever say geeked?*

I sometimes fail to tell people why I am so passionate about how the brain works. So, here it is. I learned the badass power of the human brain when I was around fourteen. Picture me: braced up, corn-rowed, and gangly. *Yes, cornrows.* My sister was hospitalized out of town for an eating disorder. My parents would spend every weekend visiting her and due to school and my grandmother's napping schedule, I was left to my own devices. My freedom quickly turned into a serious issue with terrible choices and depression. I've seen the dark alleyways of my soul. I've sat through sleepless nights ruminating on situations out of my control. Through research and a dab of therapy, I was able to understand that our brain is nothing more than an automated machine that we sometimes have to intentionally reprogram. By gaining mindfulness of what's going on in your head, you can truly upgrade your life. If this information can pull me out of depression, I'm convinced that by sharing all the brain hacks, you too can face whatever you are up against.

This book is not for you if you don't give a shit about how your brain works and have no interest in changing your life. It's not for you if you can't handle my simple approach, questionable sense of humor, and inappropriate analogies. So, if those conditions do not apply; I'm here for you. I'll hold your hand if you've dealt with a lot of negative thoughts, anxiety, or depression. I'm on your team if you are trying to better yourself by learning to tap into your full potential. I am here and will be your ride or die if you picked up this book because you're striving to be successful in business, relationships, or other areas of your life. And, well, if you are just here because you're bored or curious—I welcome you still, let me feed your curiosity with fun facts and ideas. I want to show you your power. Are you ready?

CHAPTER *One*

Why?

My kids regularly ask to partake in activities, like riding
their bikes off stairs or building a fort in the neighbor's
pricker bushes. *These are real examples.* And, of course,
my motherly answer is always *(Are you crazy?)* "No."

My nine-year-old, who could've had OJ
convicted with her impressive logical arguments,
counters, "But whyyy?"

Which drives me nuts. Like, what, kid? It's not
self-explanatory that I don't want to be tweezing
prickers out of your ass for the next twenty-four hours?
And although it drives me batty, *why* is a super
important question. My explanation assists her in
managing future discernment for similar experiences. Or
it will provide her with a reason to attend therapy when
she has a quarter-life crisis. Either way.

Your *why* is what drives you. It's what keeps you moving in the right direction. A strong *why* helps you make better choices to live your best life.[2]

Before this becomes another self-help book you skim through then throw on your shelf to collect dust only to sell in a rummage sale for 50 cents in two years—I'm on to you—I want you to establish a sound reason for *why* you are reading this book and *why* you are ready to make changes. *Why* are you sick of the way life has been going? *Why* are you over the thoughts that have been on repeat in your head? *Why* are you ready for an upgrade?

What I'm about to say is harsh. *Forgive me.* There's no easy way to say this, but you and everyone you know will be dead soon. *I know, I am a bringer of light.* Maybe 90 years from now or maybe tonight when you fall asleep. If you knew you were going to croak in approximately four hours you'd be a lot less worried about Susan in HR or how much of a jerk the guy is who didn't shovel his sidewalk. You wouldn't be sweating about your bills being late. Death is a nice reminder that most of the stuff we obsess over and stress over is pure crap.

If no other reason for a change exists, let your *why* be that you don't know how long you have here on earth and you are ready to stop wasting time. Maybe that's morbid, but it's a bit of reality I want to spring right into your pretty little face. You don't want to be dragging your life around for the next 50 years feeling like you'd rather be anywhere else when you actually COULD be somewhere else. It's possible to experience true happiness. You can have your dream job, or dream man, or dream house on your own island with piles of money protected by two English mastiffs and a housekeeper named Frankfort who wears a tux at all times and brings you the finest mimosa in those little glass flutes with your name inscribed on them first thing every morning.

I might have thought this through.

Remember that you have all the power you need in your brain, body, and soul to make whatever changes you desire. You are responsible for your own life. Perhaps your *why* is simple, you deserve more than the life you have been settling for. You are an extension of the Universe. The energy that creates worlds is inside of you, my friend. Embrace your power.

Maybe your *why* is because you don't want to feel like crap, be part of something that no longer brings you joy, or be a miserable human five years from now. Perchance if you fail to create change, misery is exactly what is going to happen. Maybe your *why* is you wouldn't want this life for your kiddos. I'm sure if you caught them settling, you would kick their butt straight into next week. So, why allow less than a stellar life for yourself?

Establishing a sound *why* keeps you driving forward, taking risks, and pushing past obstacles that block your joy. Because there will be obstacles. *Maybe disguised as those little mushroom people from Super*

Mario Brothers. Your *why* will be handy on those tough days when you'd rather feed your body to an angry group of sharks than get out of bed. For the days where you want to hide in the back of your closet, tucked in the fetal position, with a fistful of chocolate. There will be days like that. Although, this book is designed to help you reduce the number of the bad days. Your *why* helps you push through subconscious patterns, taking the more challenging route to create change rather than falling back into the familiar one.

Defining your *why* creates purpose. How do you want to measure your life? Probably not in how many episodes of *Orange is the New Black* you binge-watched.

Write it down. Tape it on your ceiling. Leave a reminder on your cell phone. Remember every single day *why* you need to make changes in your world to fast-track you into your best self.

Try this. *Fill in the blanks.*

I'm ready to change __A SITUATION__ *because this*

causes me to feel ANXIOUS . *The risk to not making*

changes is LESS CHOICES. *If I do change*

___A___, *I would feel* MORE EMPOWERED *and these*

things would be different about my life/my behavior/my

thoughts/my interactions:

__FREEDOM TO EXPLORE__ .

FREEDOM TO FINISH WHAT
WE STARTED

FREEDOM TO HELP OTHERS

FREEDOM TO LIVE FULLY

CHAPTER Two

Excuses

Now that you've created your *why* and determined the real reason you want to make changes, your brain is going to go into overdrive mode with excuses. Excuses are when you are trying to lose weight and your brain says, "I'm too busy to meal prep and grocery shop." *I'll just snack on this cupcake and maybe this Boston cream donut. Yes, definitely the donut.* Excuses are notoriously packed with "I can't," "I'm too ____ for that" (insert young, old, overweight, underweight, scared, poor, rich, etc.) Let's grab a salted caramel mocha and chat about how to get around these little buggers.

First things first, I'm asking you to take full responsibility for every part of your life, even the crappy parts. I could sit here and say, well, I am the way I am because of my parents or because I'm in a bad relationship. I hate my job. My boss is a misogynistic dickwad. I loathe being a stay-at-home mom. I could name a million and twenty reasons why I'd rather swim from Cuba than walk another day in my own shoes. But the very serious memo that I have for you is, dudes and dudettes, as *You are a Badass* author Jen Sincero says, "It's not your fault if you're fucked up. It's your fault if you stay fucked up." *Amen, sista!*

You can't control whether you had a shitty childhood or if you married a guy who turned into Hitler a year later. You can't control if you lost a limb in a tragic accident or if you were diagnosed with a debilitating disease. You can't go back and rework any aspect of the past, but you have every power in your awesome body to make changes starting right now.

If life isn't unicorns and rainbows for you—and hasn't been for a while—if you find yourself lifelessly dragging your carcass from your kid's soccer game to yoga practice, let's face it, you NEED to ditch the excuses, put the reins back in your hands, and spice up your life. Or listen to the Spice Girls. *Probably the first option, mixed with a dash of the second option. Tell me what you want, what you really, really want.*

My biggest excuse for not being more successful or not becoming the author I always dreamed I would be was that I became pregnant when I was twenty years old. Having children young takes a lot of focus away from your future. Not to mention, I had little in terms of support. Plenty of people in my immediate environment, including professors and family members, practically begged me to drop out of college. *I didn't.*

I often envisioned my life without kids. *What? We are being so honest right now.* I saw myself being so much more successful than I am in my current situation. Single, non-mom me would have been a doctor. A doctor of psychology, not one who hangs out with people with weird rashes. This book would've been finished minimum six years ago. Non-mom me could've even discovered something amazing studying humans in a village in Uganda. But alas, I didn't apply to do more schooling because the cost of daycare was destroying every ounce of my soul and bank account. It's not like you can go off to work or school and leave your kids under a bridge somewhere. *There, there honey, you just hang out under this bridge and there might be some fish in that creek over there if you get hungry. Well, off to work.* Life doesn't work like that.

Here's the reality of the situation: Having children has gifted me with many skills and personality traits that I simply didn't possess beforehand. Motherhood has forced me to be more organized, improving my time management skills. I swear I can get more done in one hour than most people do in a week. Being a mom has made me more compassionate, loving, and understanding of other people. I'm constantly bettering myself and driving my ambition to show my girls the art of working hard and following your dreams. *Plus, my kids are so freaking cool.*

If I didn't have kids, I'd create a different excuse. I used to work three jobs before becoming a parent, plus do extra activities like theater productions and an impressive amount of tanning. I never thought I had time to do anything like laundry or chasing down my goals. I know now pre-kid me, that whiny little princess, could've done anything with her spare time. Mom-me found out the hard way: When you are keeping humans alive, time is a precious commodity.

Excuses keep us comfortable. We make excuses because we are afraid or because we truly need better life management and organization skills. Ask yourself: What's your excuse? Why haven't you left that job or situation? Why don't you have more fun with your life? Where in your life are you lying to yourself?

The truth is we pretend we can't do things when in reality, we have endless possibilities. These potentialities may be challenging, they may force you to get creative, but there are multiple options available. Don't block yourself in with the whole "it's not possible" thing. The infallibility is you can start a business or find your dream job. A healthier relationship is possible. Your bank account can be less terrifying.

You don't have to swipe and pray. Maybe you're scared

it will be too much work or that upgrading isn't possible

for you. Perhaps, you're terrified that it won't be what

you want or will be a mistake in the long run. Are you

nervous that change will be difficult or uncomfortable

and you won't be able to handle it? Real change can

happen the minute you acknowledge fear is the piece

stopping you, not the impossibility. We can work with

fear. So, ditch your excuses at the door. You are the only

one responsible for your happiness, no one is going to

walk in and create your dream life for you.

The first time I realized I was blocking myself

with excuses was when I read one of Danielle LaPorte's

books. The a-ha moment wasn't even from the content

of this book, previously I had admired the success of

people who didn't have kids. I figured of course they

had time to write books; they didn't have to cut

fingernails and wake up at 5 a.m. with someone

breathing over them demanding they play Barbies. But

Danielle was different. She had a child. She knew. She got it. And she busted her ass to get her book out into the world, self-published and all. Her example wrecked my excuse. I recognized I wasn't creating time to write my own book because maybe being an author just wasn't that important to me. *Gasp!* But I had dreamt about writing my own book series since I was a little girl. Yeah? But I wasn't willing to work for the feeling of holding my own book in my hands. I wasn't willing to wake up and go to sleep writing. I only wrote when I felt inspired and had a couple of minutes to jot down my thoughts. I never made time to pursue my passions. Look for examples of people who have similar situations as you who are totally crushing it.

You will make time for the things that you deem important. If you aren't making time for what you love, ask yourself why not? What happens if you begin to follow your dreams? Do you feel guilty or worried about what people will think?

If you want to begin assessing what you truly value, check your bank account and your calendar. Where do you spend your time and where do you spend your money? Considering time and money are a form of energy, exploring where and how you use this energy can help you keep tabs on your priorities and where you might be wasting your energy. The direction of your energy drives your life. Many of us are so accustomed to saying phrases like, "I don't have time" or "I'm too busy," to the point we really believe it. *You have as many hours in the day as Beyoncé!* How much time do you spend sitting on the couch or scrolling through social media? How much time do you waste on Netflix? Make time for the activities, goals, and dreams that are most important to you.

Try this. *Fill in the blanks.*

My biggest excuse is LACK OF TIME : ENERGY

What I'm actually afraid of is SUCCEEDING

Overcoming this fear would mean REWIRING MY BRAIN HOW WILL IT IMPACT MY FAMILY

21

I spend the majority of my time and energy

on _BOYS, TOM-TV, WASTE_

I'd be more successful if I spent my time and energy

on _TALKING TO OTHERS_

My first step is to _CREATE A TIME_
SCHEDULE
WITH BLOCKS OF
TIME DETERMINED

CHAPTER *Three*

Perception

One time I was in New York City for a friend's birthday.
We had been out on the town and stumbled into what
can be best described as an ecstasy-driven, freak version
of a burlesque show. Inside, a—*can I call her a
stripper?*—sat her bare ass on my coat. When a stripper
or anyone sits on your coat wearing nothing but a G-
string you might need an extra drink. Since it was 20
degrees outside and I'd need to eventually put my coat
back on, I did the only rational thing and consumed four
more glasses of straight Kentucky bourbon.

The show came to a close around 3 a.m., and we
were beat, so I attempted to hail a cab in the way that
only an out-of-towner can do. I awkwardly stepped into
the road and threw my hand up in a seizure sort of way
as one flew by—quickly pulling my arm back in deep

rejection. If you ever hail a cab in New York City, the key is to act confident, like you know what you're doing. *Important fact: I did not know what I was doing.* As I stepped back on the sidewalk, I noticed a parked limo and jokingly said, "Hey guys, our ride is here." The driver popped his head out and said, "Do you want a ride?" *Why yes, yes, we do.* We eagerly scrambled into the back of the limo, giving him the address to our swanky little hotel in downtown Manhattan. This man offered us champagne as we were whisked off towards our place in the most *Sex and the City* way possible. We cranked up the music and lunged towards our destination as a dance party broke out in the back of the limo. *I think this is how Carrie Bradshaw must've felt.*

Picture my two besties and I, rhythmically flopping our arms drunkenly in the air as we sang off-key at the top of our lungs to early 2000s' Britney. But then, I began to notice we were driving a very different way back to the hotel. Nothing like the road we took on our way there in the taxi. Our badass limo was suddenly swerving under tunnels and through some sketchy areas of town that had windows dressed with bars across them. The occasional flash of police lights that entered through the limo windows injected an unsettling feeling in the air. I looked at my best friend, Sam, with the sudden, "Think we are maybe getting kidnapped and sold to be sex slaves?" kind of look. *I knew this limo thing was too good to be true.*

The fun settled down and our hearts raced with anticipation as we tracked the limo on our GPS and flipped on the "find a friend" feature on our phones, *just in case.* Still slightly jamming, yet worried that we'd be transferred to something out of the movie *Taken.* I could see it clearly. I'd be forced to stand in the middle of a rotating circle while men puffing imported cigars placed bets on me and my friends. Not to kill the suspense but I will tell you this story ends up ridiculously uneventful— no cigars, no rotating circle, and definitely no Liam Neeson. I nearly kissed the urine-covered New York City pavement when we arrived unscathed at our destination. *I guess shortcuts and beating traffic are also cool.* Realizing you aren't getting kidnapped is a pretty rad feeling.

There I was, free as a pay-it-forward cup of coffee, recognizing nothing had changed about the situation except my perception of it. In reality, I could've stayed in full-on, drunk-fun party mode, but my twisted little brain had turned this into a suspense novel. My perception of the situation had shifted even when it wasn't necessary, ruining the entire experience.

We have our own perceptions of the world as well as shifting perceptions throughout each day and even moment-to-moment experiences. How we view the world creates how we feel on a regular basis. Positive perceptions of our life and situations lead to positive feelings and often positive experiences. Negative perceptions create negative feelings and often negative experiences.[3]

I feel like I need to roll out the red carpet for this one. Guys, this is the Beyoncé of concepts to understand.

Perception is everything. **This is how you, as an individual, view, filter, and assign meaning to the world which then drives your feelings, behaviors, and interactions.** *Get out your highlighter.* Perception is how you make sense of what's going on around you and within you, which is completely unique of anyone and everyone else. Your perception is a filtering system that scans and interprets situations and experiences. Your brain searches your external world only for matching information, validating your internal thoughts and beliefs.

Think of your perception as the bouncer at a club you own. The bouncer's job is to only allow people you are familiar with or want to be familiar with inside, rejecting anyone who doesn't fit the description. Your perception functions similarly, constantly on the search to allow in only ideas and examples matching what we already know or believe to be true, completely missing, rejecting, or critically scanning any opposing evidence.

Our perceptions are powerful but we must question them because they are not always accurate. For example, I really love collecting crystals and precious stones. Envision me, late summer, skipping pebbles across the lake with my daughters, when I spot a shiny rock. My eyes light up as I think to myself, "What a special rock, that looks like a black tourmaline." My excitement overcomes me as I run up to grab this very special stone, wrapping my fingers around this mushy and warm ro...wait a second, what is this? My panic and pure disgust set in when the realization that what I'm grabbing is not a precious stone, but extra-wet animal poo. *I guess the wetness gives it a shine?* Moral of the story? Your perception, which you think is great and correct, might actually be shit. *See what I did there?*

It's as simple and uncomplicated as this: In life, you see what you believe. You become the thoughts you think about. You see in the world what you believe to be true. Perception begins forming from the time you are born. It's comprised of every experience good and bad, every thought and impression of every person you have interacted with. Your parents, your community, your friends, and your cultural expectations all have starring roles in how you view yourself, and your world. They've told you what is right, what is wrong, what is normal, and it's likely that you've believed them. Because your perception has been forming for a while, without being questioned. Your world view could easily be comprised of really old, unhelpful thoughts or ideas that are more outdated than floral wallpaper and a shag carpet. *I mean, do you still need to be leery of girls named Ashley because of that time in first grade when an Ashley locked you in her playhouse?* Instead of saying, "Hey, this wallpaper has way too much going on. This pattern no longer works for me," we accept the old wallpaper as reality, we don't even question it. This ugly-ass wallpaper (our perception) is now the system that we use to help us understand the world. *Nobody wants ugly wallpaper dictating their life experience.*

Understanding that our mind is forced to see what we believe, is so important. For example, if we think no one likes us we will notice the people who look down and away more than those who are trying to make eye contact or smile, because that fits with our perceptual view that we are unlikeable. The smiling, friendly folks will seem irrelevant. *They couldn't possibly like me; they probably were just thinking about a swimming pool of Jell-O. Who wouldn't be happy thinking about that?*

In contrast, if we believe everyone loves us we are more likely to notice the people who are smiling and holding the door open for us. Anyone we perceive to be scowling or in a bad mood is just in a bad mood, which has nothing to do with us. *Obvi.* One belief shapes everything. Correcting unhealthy perceptions is as simple as becoming aware of how your thought or perception makes you feel. If the perception feels good, keep it! If it feels bad, explore if there is an alternative way to view this situation.

You can learn about your perception by studying your thoughts and beliefs. What do you believe about the world in general? Is it a terrifying place? Is it always raining in Philadelphia? If you believe the world is a bad place, your brain will filter out the positives to find the negatives, the trauma, the major scary events. For example, my mother could find anything to be afraid of. Last time she came to visit, I went to get in the shower and noticed my bath mat was missing. She then tells me that she heard bath mats can be a host for bacteria including flesh-eating viruses. *Face palm. Stop watching the news.*

Same idea goes for connection. What do you believe about relationships? Do they always fail or is it happily ever after? If you believe that relationships don't work, then you will find relationship tension. You'll discover yourself surrounded by people who also have failing relationships or are bitter about love. You will see it on the news, read it in the tabloids, "Oh, that Angelina and Brad story was just heartbreaking, but nothing really lasts." What you believe is exactly what you will see. Despite examples of wonderful marriages, if you don't believe relationship happiness exists, you will never see it. You will never fully acknowledge positive relationships as reality, only as outliers. Mistakes. Exceptions. If you accept them as reality, then you would have to admit you are wrong, which will create anxiety within you. *No one likes to be wrong.*

Per second, our environment has about 400 billion bits of information trying to get our brains' attention, according to *E Squared* author Pam Grout.[4] *Holy Eff.* Which means that our efficient brain has to scan so we only see what's relevant and matches our beliefs, otherwise we would be in information overload! Truth is created by what you believe and the evidence you gather, along the way further validating that belief as true. Just because you believe a specific thought or idea, doesn't make it fact.

When I was little I was the world's pickiest eater. Any slight adjustment away from my diet of chicken tenders and hot dogs would be under a seriously critical eye. Unfortunately for my sensitive taste buds, my dad was a great hunter. I could be scarred any Sunday morning by walking into a half-gutted deer dangling from the ceiling of our garage. As much as I'm not a fan of hunting, I will say that my dad used/consumed everything he hunted. Which means I was regularly offered venison for dinner. *I, however, boldly refused. I mean c'mon I saw this "food's" eyeballs. We shared a moment. I can't see its eyeballs and then consume the poor animal.*

I spent my life avoiding venison. The face-to-face dangling deer encounters were too real for me. Last summer, I was attending a picnic with my dad's family when I was offered venison once more. My response was, "I have never tried deer meat and don't intend to start," when my dad whipped his head around and blurted out, "Of course, you have." This is the part where I choked on and classily spit out the honey dew of my fruit salad. *I beg your pardon?* He proceeds to tell me I ate mostly hot dogs growing up, which he made out of venison. Lying to me was the only way they could get me to eat the deer meat. My perception was that I was consuming hot dogs, not my *deer*-est friends. *My whole childhood was a lie.*

An important question to ask yourself is, is this thought even real? Are there other possibilities of what could be true? Am I perceiving this situation in a way that is creating anxiety, sadness, or anger? We create a lot of unnecessary emotions from grand illusions of our perceptual world. Meaning, we get real worked up about stuff that is probably not even true. *If you've ever thought your boyfriend was cheating on you because he was late coming home from work, only to find he stopped to buy you flowers and hibachi take-out, you know what I'm talking about.*

I want you to consider this is *your* movie. Your perception controls whether it's a horror film or a romantic comedy. You are M. Night Shyamalan directing the show through the perceptions you created.

Don't make everyone die or live in a weird deceptive, gated village with a scary pig head instead of seeing a modernized world.

If you want a better life, you have to double-check some of your perceptions. Are you making yourself a victim to the world? Are you looking for the ailments or bad experiences? Are you negating the good experiences and positives that come your way? Are you trying to succeed in an area of your life that you truly don't have faith that you can succeed in? Gaining awareness of how we are viewing the world is the first big step into living a better life. What you look for, you will see.

Try this. *Consider your personal view of the following areas of life. Are your perceptions of each area helpful or unhelpful? Positive or negative? What type of experience will you receive if you are filtering through that particular perception? Fill in the blanks.*

My view of the world is _____ POSITIVE _____

CHANGING

My view of relationships is _MEN · EASY, WOMEN TIRED_

My view of finances or financial freedom is

ROLLER COASTER

My view of myself is _KIND, LOVING, NOT ENOUGH_

My view of my health is _NEEDS WORK_

*Other areas you might explore include your views on
success, spirituality, weight/fitness, fun, politics, travel,
areas of the world, family and friends, personal growth,
and community.*

CHAPTER *Four*

Thoughts

Consider for a moment how ridiculous our thoughts are. We have a constant flow of *what-ifs, I-cants, maybes,* and *how's* racing rapidly around our skulls. We spend the majority of our spare time in our heads, thinking—no matter what subject has caught our attention. Our brains are meaning-makers, designed to make sense of the world around us, and are churning at a rapid rate, desperate for a problem to solve.

If I'm not thinking about how many clients I did or didn't book, I'm thinking about how I'm screwing up my kids by yelling at them over a mess they left in the living room. I've caught myself obsessing over how much I spent on groceries. *Those organic sunshine raspberries, although amazing, were almost $2 more than the non-organic. Maybe I should've just purchased* *non-organic, like, what is truly organic these days anyway?* I've felt my face flush red with embarrassment an entire year later, remembering my niece's first birthday party when I had my dress tucked up into my underwear, flashing my thong to all of my sister's co-workers.

Our brains are constantly moving but it's typically not day-dreaming of a vacation in Malibu or that brand new Tesla Model X we hope to acquire in the near future. We rarely future-cast a happily ever after. Our time is often focused on what if happiness never finds us, or what if in five years we can't stand our significant other. We mentally self-sabotage before we have the possibility to be optimistic about a situation. Our natural focus on worrying isn't entirely our fault. Our mind is designed to prepare ourselves for shit to hit the fan. *Not that preplanning our doom has ever alleviated any sensations when the doom actually shows up, but hey, let's panic anyway!* Our brains are machines that are built for survival, they are made to scan for safety.[5]

These days we are less concerned about a saber-toothed tiger running off with little Jimmy, so we put energy into stupid things like paranoia over our self-concept, our professional image, or the broccoli we just discovered in our teeth. *C'mon, no one was going to tell me?* Here's the thing. **Your perception is formed and shaped by thoughts. Your thoughts create your feelings and your feelings drive your behaviors.[6]**

Easy peasy lemon squeezy flowchart:

Thoughts -> Feelings -> Behaviors

At the root of everything are your thoughts. We hold beliefs. Beliefs are only thoughts you keep thinking over and over again and have developed evidence for. That's it. That's why you can hold up a blue crayon and call it blue. Someone showed you the color blue, showing you the color over and over again while repeating that very word. Now, let's say you were held hostage in a basement for most of your life and maybe you only interacted with one other person, we will call him Frank. And let's pretend when Frank showed you a blue crayon, instead of saying blue, he called it magoo. *Maybe he didn't know any better, or maybe Frank is just a vindictive asshole. We will never know!* Now every time that you look at that color, you say to yourself, "Oh, that's magoo." No one ever told you most people call it blue so you now know it as magoo.

The blissful day comes when you are rescued from this hostage-situation and released into society when a stranger comes up to you on the street and says to you, "The sky is so blue today." Your brain gets all confused and your body feels weird. Why on earth did this person call it blue? Clearly, they are confused. So, you say, "You mean, magoo?" He looks at you like you have two heads and you part ways. Someone just challenged what you thought and now your insides feel weird but, good news, your brain will naturally write him off as a lunatic because his thought was so different than yours.

Now you might say to me, "Nichole, let's face it, that analogy is ridiculous." But my point is, thoughts and beliefs are ridiculous. That's why we can have a world that is half Democrats, half Republicans, and half people who don't give a heck about politics because we all believe our views are the correct views. *I know that's too many halves but I'm a psychology major, not a math major.*

Remember, our thoughts and beliefs develop based on what we are repeatedly told, hear, or experience. This includes all of the information you've gathered throughout your lifetime from the towns, the cities, the schools, and parents who all have had something to say about every detail of your life. This includes friends, family, bad or good experiences, mentors, and perfect strangers. When they say you become whom you are around, it's 100% true. Try holding completely different thoughts, beliefs, or even feelings, from the people in your immediate existence. The discrepancy will make your skin crawl. Try being happy around people who are sad. You will feel the contrast immediately.

If you haven't caught on, we LOVE to be right and we hate anything that challenges the way we feel about things, which is why we are so quick to dismiss information that doesn't match what we already believe. Accepting alternate information would create *cognitive dissonance*.[7] Cognitive dissonance is where information in our environment is contradictory to our beliefs— creating anxiety and forcing us to make a choice to label the presenting external information as bogus or accept it as a new truth, in order to keep internal consistency.

Repeating the same or similar thoughts over and over is how we form our beliefs. Our beliefs create our perception. That is exactly how we filter our world, picking through our universe for evidence which supports what we already believe. I know I'm being repetitive. But the brain remembers what is repeated,

IF YOU CHANGE YOUR THOUGHTS &
BELIEFS, YOU CHANGE EVERYTHING

whether it's true or not true. Which means the total crap you have developed in your head about not being good enough or never going far in life or what you can or can't have are ludicrous. These bullshit thoughts are simply untruths that you've repeated and developed enough evidence for to engrain as a belief. The reality is if you change your thoughts and beliefs, you change EVERYTHING—including your entire limiting perception. Great news! You can believe in yourself. You can feel better. You can have whatever it is you want. *Boom! Magic!*

Changing your mind starts with choosing a better thought. You wouldn't stand in front of a display of peaches and pick the dirty, dented, smooshed up peach, right? *I hope not, that's sort of weird.* You'd pick the best peach. The gloriously juicy one, plump with sugary goodness. Choose your thoughts like that too. Pick thoughts that make you excited about your life, self, and your future. Favor thoughts that feel good when you think or say them.

If anything can be true and we are simply gathering evidence, then decide you are worthy. Decide your life is kick ass, amazeballs, full of exciting opportunities and quality people. Remember, when you decide your value, your brain will naturally start looking for matching information in your world.

If you've caught yourself on a slippery slope of shitty thoughts, it's okay. Our brains are silly like that sometimes. Your only job is to be aware of crappy thoughts and how they make you feel. You can decide in that moment to offer forgiveness to yourself and simply pick out a better thought. You can choose to refocus your energy on gratitude or joy. Or you can start over tomorrow. *Some days are awash and our best defense is to try again tomorrow. I won't judge you. I pinky-promise.*

The risk of not controlling your thoughts is huge. Your thoughts directly control your emotions. Each thought produces a feeling. You get the opportunity to control how you feel through your

GRATITUDE AND JOY

thoughts. A life of negative thoughts creates negative emotions followed by negative interactions and experiences. Not correcting your unhelpful thoughts leads to a life of limitation and often fear.

Anything can be true in our heads if we acquire enough evidence. Ask yourself, is this thought true? Is the thought helpful? What would I rather think about? What feeling is this thought creating?

Try this. *I want you to think of a situation that is the center of your focus right now. Fill in the blanks.*

Situation: DREAM / HOPE

What I am thinking about it:

UNSUPPORTIVE PEOPLE

How this thought makes me feel:

ANGRY B/C PEOPLE ARE UNKIND

Is the thought true or helpful?

NOT HELPFUL

What thought can I try instead that might feel a little better? BE GRATEFUL FOR FAMILY & FRIENDS WHO DO SUPPORT YOU

Is there a different perspective?

YES! ALWAYS!

CHAPTER *Five*

Intention

Your thoughts are powerful and they guide perception, which means by being intentional in choosing your thoughts you can begin to see different information in your world and feel better emotionally.

This is GREAT news! Now we know we can choose to feel better. An *intention* is simply a thought that contains an outcome we wish to have or feel. Your intention might be as simple as, "Today is a great day" or "I feel so confident going into this presentation." Now you might be saying, "Every day is not a great day, Nichole." I hear you. However, simply saying, "Today is a great day" improves your perceptual filters—which means your brain will begin to look for evidence in your environment to match your new thought. You are more likely to notice situations, experiences, and people in alignment with how you feel. You may notice the guy who helped you out in the copy room instead of zoning in on the fact that the copy machine broke. You may notice positive feedback over the one critical review.

An intention is a map asking your brain to find a route to your destination. Setting an intention, in your head, out loud, or on paper, immediately demands your brain to start looking both internally and externally for possibilities. Being intentional about choosing better thoughts can help you become more successful, communicate better, develop confidence, manage stress and negative emotions, and become more present. *So basically, kick major ass.*

I want you to think of every thought as having its own search party. When you think or speak a thought declaring you can't find or have what you are looking for, the gates come down trapping the search party in a small jail cell. *Now all they can do is sit around playing poker and drinking beer.* If you change your intention to something like, "The answer is clear to me," the search party fuels up with Red Bull, turn on their headlamps, and scan all the areas of your mind and external world for evidence to match your intention.

You can set an intention for anything and everything. It's like collaborating with your brain, letting your mind know your expectations. You can create an intention around what kind of day you want to have. You can devise an intention for how you'd like to feel. Consider the impact of repeating, "I am so tired." Your body has no choice but to look for symptomatic evidence. You can create an intention for how you'd like a certain situation to go or how you want to feel during the experience. "I am calm, cool, and collected when speaking on stage to hundreds of listeners." You can set an intention for your career. "I am the top performer on my sales team for this quarter. Selling comes easy. I even score a bonus!" You can set an intention for relationships. "I feel seen, loved, and supported in my romantic relationship." You can set an intention for opening your heart and mind to see from a different

perspective. Your power is unlimited and the only

requirement is awareness and mindfulness of your

thoughts. Practicing intention-setting frequently will

allow the magical aspects of the power of your mind to

become clear.

Setting intentions is a great way to rewire your

brain from negative to positive. In order for your

intention to really create new neural pathways, you must

feel it. Without feeling, you're not making the full

connection with your brain. If you've repeated an

intention over and over that you have absolutely no

connection to, the impact isn't as strong.

Help your brain believe the thought by scaling

the affirmation back to a thought you are at least willing

to believe. For example, if you've decided that rather

than thinking you absolutely suck at your sales job

you're going to set the intention to be the top sales

person in your company, your brain might try to fight

you. Believing you're top in sales is too different a

thought to what you've worked so hard to believe (that you suck), too fast. Try scaling it back. Can you be top in your district? Can you do ten more sales than last month? Scale back until what you're wanting to improve feels possible. From there, you can build onto your intention once your belief and confidence grow and you begin to see evidence to confirm your new belief.

You must tell your brain what you want it to see. Changing your brain requires you to collaborate with it. The more frequently you encourage your mind to feel good, the more you will see these perceptions reflected in your external world. The better you will feel every single day! You have the power.

Try this. *Before going to bed tonight, set an intention* *for how you want to feel tomorrow when you wake up. Create your own intention or use mine:* "I wake up every morning feeling energized, happy, and productive. Everything is always working out for me and

I have more than enough time to do all that I wish to do in the morning and throughout my day."

CHAPTER *Six*

Word Choice

Some people don't like that I curse like a sailor. *It's worse in person.* My potty-mouth is not something I am proud of. However, growing up I was never in trouble for subtly sprinkling swear words throughout my vocabulary. A dash of "damn" here, a fickle "F-bomb" there. Swear words simply do not mean as much to me nor do they feel intensely negative. In all honesty, I find swearing to be a bit fun. *I promise I'm an adult.*

I mention my love of cursing for a reason. Words have massive power, especially pertaining to how we feel about ourselves and the world.[8] The weight of words develops power or lacks power depending on how they were used during our development. For example, if you were severely punished every time you swore, I imagine my fondness for profanity is reaching a level of disgust for you.

Uncovering which words have power versus which words take your power away, can be useful in both managing emotional reactivity and amplifying your intentions. Knowledge of word choice can even help you move on quicker through tough situations by decreasing negative emotions, detaching you from unhealthy situations or past hurts. *Which sounds pretty rad, right?*

I once heard a story about a man, we will call him Tom, who was on a safari somewhere in the Amazon rainforest. Good ol' Tommy was accompanied by a couple of other tourists exploring the beauty of draped vines, gorgeous plants, and unusual wildlife. Two hours into the late afternoon tour, the small van broke down, dead-center of the rainforest.

As the guide called for help, the sun began to set. Tom panicked, knowing the darkness of the Amazon housed the most dangerous creatures. As the majority of the tourists freaked the hell out, one of the women seemed unbothered by the potentially life-threatening scenario. She remained calm, pointing out the beauty in the moonlight and positively reflected on the rest of the day. The man grew more and more upset. How could she not understand the seriousness of the situation? Was she a moron? His fear grew into anger. Why would the guide company send them out on a broken vehicle? He was pissed. He proceeded to tell himself just how upset he was, building and growing the intensity of his distraught feelings. He was going to sue those mother-effers for all they were worth, if he ever made it back!

Meanwhile, the woman remained calm, cool, and collected, noting the experience as a slight inconvenience rather than a tragedy. All was well until a jaguar leapt through the open window, brutally mauling the man who was angry and bitching. *I'm kidding. I made that up, but getting eaten by a jaguar seems like appropriate karma.*

This story is not just an example of how word choice drives emotions, but also how two people can view the same situation in completely opposite ways.

It's impossible to move out of a crappy mindset by using the same words that got you there. Using "pissed" and "upset" will leave you pissed and upset. The woman, on the other hand, used the word "inconvenience" and expressed her gratitude for the day. Her search for positives lessened the emotional impact, creating less distress in a tricky situation.

You can manage your own emotions in difficult situations by being mindful of what words you are using and how you are talking yourself. You see, negative emotions like worry or anger, do not improve or change the situation or outcome. They only create emotional distress during the experience. At the end of the day, Tom was still ravaged by a jaguar and wasted the last few hours of his life in a pissy mood. Or would have, if that story were real.

I was recently chatting with a friend who was experiencing a difficult time transitioning from a recent break-up. "He destroyed me! I am so devastated," she exclaimed. "You can't give him that power," I replied. "Destroyed and devastated are both negative, powerful words. The more power you give your situation and this break-up, the more emotions you will have to wade through, prolonging your ability to heal and move on." By using heavy words, she was giving her power away. Consider the weight of your words, negative or positive. Lessen the blow of a challenging circumstance by choosing words that have less emotion behind them. How differently would my friend have felt if instead of "devastating" she described the break-up as "a small setback", "an annoyance", or "a bother."

The same can be said about positive, powerful words. At one point, starting my business, I had a mentor who was a total powerhouse. When she walked in the room, you could feel her presence bringing confidence to each interaction. She was well-spoken and sure of herself. I, on the other hand, was not. I didn't know what the hell I was doing running a business. In fact, I struggled finding words to tell others what my business even offered. My elevator speech was comprised of a confusing over-explanation, downplaying my expertise.

Every time I met up with my mentor, her power was clear. Powerhouse became a word representing confidence, poise, and an energy that demanded attention. I began to use the word to describe myself. "I am a powerhouse," I'd repeat while doing mundane activities like brushing my teeth or driving to work. *I mean, why not me? Why can't I be a powerhouse?*

I've got to be honest. At first, this intention and affirmation felt like bullshit. But after a few days of dedication, I could feel the burst of energy pour in, my confidence ramp-up, and a feeling of badassery consume me as I completed the intention. Use the power of words to improve yourself, your view of the world, your emotional reaction, and your ability to heal. Pay attention to the positive and negative power of the words

you choose. Make sure your words are helping you

move forward instead of keeping you stuck.

Try this. *Fill in the blanks.*

What word(s) makes you feel

powerful? _I AM STRONG. I AM ENOUGH._

What word(s) takes away your power?

"YOU NEED" "YOU HAVE TOO'

In what situation are you using negative powerful

words? _____

Write an intention using powerful words:

_____

I AM A POWERHOUSE
WITH VIBRANCY.

CHAPTER Seven

Focus

Remember when we talked about checking your bank account and calendar? Where is the majority of your energy going? Being focused is vital to making progress and improving our lives. If we lack mindfulness in our focus, we risk wasting a ton of time on an idea or problem that may never positively add to our overall experience.

Our cavemen relatives were all, like, "I hope there's enough food to feed my family. I hope a mammoth doesn't come in and spear grandma." And here we are, like, "Oh man, I hope Becky isn't wearing the same outfit as me." *You know, Becky with the good hair. Why is her hair so much better anyway? It's like she has more money so she can afford a better stylist. I wish I had more money. I never have money to do anything with.* Our focus can create an emotional downward spiral staircase real fast. Whatever we are focusing our thoughts on, more similar thoughts and feelings join in.

Have you ever had a bad break-up? The type where you mope around the house wearing their hoodie sans showering for a couple days? *It's okay; you don't have to admit it. We've all been there.* You might have been so focused on rereading their texts in an attempt to understand what happened, you declined an invite to a fun event. Showers and eating anything other than stale pizza went out the window while you were busy wondering why you weren't worth keeping. The entire situation, which is really only a fraction of your life, consumed days, weeks, or possibly years of your mental focus—inducing sadness or anger. Moving out of these emotions feels impossible.

The truth is, we always have access to a new feeling or state of being. For example, let's say your ex called and wanted to meet up, you'd likely be filled with a burst of hopeful energy pushing you to shower or clean your apartment. Shifting our focus only takes one second's notice to take our thoughts from fearful and sad to empowered and excited. Which means you have access to better feelings at all times, you just have to hone in on them by shifting your focus.[9] You can even access better states or emotions just by recalling a time you felt happy, excited, or proud.

Not to say that you aren't allowed to have negative emotions or grief. You are. A normal part of life is dealing with or healing from tough experiences, we just don't want to live there. *Shitty feelings are not meant to be a vacation home on the Cape.* Be mindful of the amount of time you spend in a negative emotion. Redirecting your focus to an area of your life that makes you feel good, or that you have control over, will move you towards joy.

Creating awareness of where your focus is, helps you decide if what pulled your focus off your path is worth your time. We focus a lot of our time on our insecurities and the areas in our life that suck. *Since when do I have fine lines? Oh my god, my lips are even wrinkled. I have old-people lips!* We focus a lot of time on worries that in the long term won't matter. Redirecting your focus is as easy as consciously choosing to focus your thoughts elsewhere.

You can also use the power of questions. Your brain is forced to answer the questions you ask it. Instead of asking yourself why you weren't worth keeping, ask yourself what you want your standards to be in your next relationship. Instead of asking why you didn't get picked for that job or school, ask what you learned or how you can improve your resume or interview skills moving forward. Refocusing can take you from self-loathing to taking action.

What are you missing while focusing on how the government is ruining our nation? Are you sacrificing your joy by pouring your energy into desperate, low feeling thoughts or situations that you have no control over? This doesn't mean you should simply avoid the deeper, darker subjects; you should make a pro-active decision to not stay in the dark. If you can't find a way to be active about a worrisome situation, move along or give yourself 15 minutes only to think about it per day.

"Worry time"[10] is a cognitive psychology tool that recommends you redirect a concern or worry as it arises to a designated time, like 5 p.m. As the thought arises, you should say to yourself, "Nope, I can only think about this at 5 p.m." Only at your designated worry time can you be anxious about this particular concern. For a whole 15 minutes, you must sit there and utilize that time solely to fret. Once your 15 minutes is up, you should find a calming or distracting activity and redirect your energy elsewhere until the next designated "worry time." This practice trains your brain to refocus and gain relief from intruding thoughts.

When you focus your energy and mind on building something great or even feeling great, we create more situations that feel good. It's like rolling a snowball down a hill, you build glorious momentum. When you focus your energy on things that aren't working, you create more situations that feel bad. Choose wisely.

Try this. *Fill in the blanks.*

What do you spend the majority of your day focused on?

BOYS, HomE, BIZ, ME

What do you regularly worry about?

LISTS OF TASK RELATED TO ALL, $

What could you change your focus to, that would bring you joy or make you feel successful?

ADDING GRATITUDE

_____

CHAPTER Eight

Limits

I was born with a plethora of health concerns. My weak, tiny infant body was hospitalized shortly after I arrived. Luckily, many of the health issues subsided over the years, but complications remained, including severe asthma and chronic lung infections.

Health issues meant a lifetime of the word "no". "No, you can't play outside, it's too cold, your lungs can't handle the Upstate New York weather." "You're going to need to sit out in gym today, the wheezing is getting worse." "Don't even consider joining a sports team, your lungs can't commit." My parents took the doctors anti-activity advice very seriously. Let's just say my doctors advised against anything appearing fun. My lungs improved gradually as I grew older, giving me permission to expand my preset limits, barely. *I joined a softball team. I wasn't very good.* However, when I approached my twenties my lungs began boxing lessons, taking me down with a right hook. Battling chronic bronchitis soon consumed my life.

Now if you've never had bronchitis—it sucks. Imagine trying to breathe with pillows over your face. Everything, including laughing, makes you cough. *You definitely don't want to laugh.* Once you start coughing, good luck stopping. The coughing is exhausting and keeps you up all night, not only do you feel like crap but combined with the sleep deprivation you look like crap.

At one point, I developed a new bout of bronchitis almost immediately after getting over the last stint. *I was just a hacking, phlegm-producing machine. Super sexy.* Meanwhile, all of my twenty-something friends were using their fancy lungs to do cool activities like run marathons. I'd envy stories of training in groups, crossing the finish lines, medals, a post-race brew followed by a carb-filled meal. I was fifty-shades of green. *Jealous as hell.* I wanted to run. I couldn't because of my lungs. Doctors would surely advise against it.

For as many problems as I was born with, I also came equipped with a curiosity that just won't quit. On one of the days when my lungs were feeling okay, I had this urge. What if I just lightly jogged a quarter-mile? I laced up my sneakers and stepped outside. I did a slow jog, breaking that quarter of a mile. I'd love to say it was so easy, but if I'm being honest, the racing heart and burning in my lungs had me convinced I was going to die. Yet, a weird glow of pride loomed over me the rest of the day.

The next day the pride fogged my memory enough for me to try my jog again, even slower. I followed this slow pattern for two weeks. Over the course of two weeks, I experienced zero lung infections. I discovered running challenges strengthened my lungs. Fast forward five years later, I run between two to five miles every morning. I have entered numerous 5ks, competed in 8ks and 10ks, I've pushed myself through an 11-mile mud run obstacle course. But most importantly, I haven't had any major infections in my lungs since.

People are going to set limits for you. Experts. Family. Intelligent individuals who love you. Only you can decide what your limits are. If you don't like your restrictions, push on them. Maybe surpassing your limits really just starts as a "what if" game. What if just this once I [insert limitation push here]? Nudging your limits could begin by taking it slow and building upon your small successes. Most importantly, decide the created limit does NOT have to be your truth. Consider that what's on the other side of our limit is worth trying for.

Few limits are real and physical, most limits are just thoughts, meaning we can change them. Some limits will feel impossible but remember, there are anomalies every day that defy preset limitations. If you don't believe me look at the fact we have electricity and humankind has landed on the moon. Imagine the first time someone pointed up to the moon and shouted, "Someone should stand on that moon!" People probably thought the idea and person was insane. Yet, because of that insanity, the moon has been stood on! There are currently people walking around who were told they'd never walk again. Hearing when they were told they would never hear. "Impossible" happenings occur daily.

Not everyone is going to agree with your ideas and thoughts or support you. The world will give you the chance to quit and go back to safety every single day. You have to be the one to believe fiercely in your own possibility. You must boldly surpass your own limitations. The alternative is living a life of safety and playing by the rules, settling for less. Great structures, discoveries, and inventions wouldn't exist if limits were not eliminated. Don't let your life be any different. Decide for yourself. Push your own barriers and see exactly what you are capable of. Be willing to go at it alone. Trust yourself and your intuition when it comes to making your dream life happen. Your soul knows what

you are capable of, decide which boundaries you are
ready to surpass.

Try this. *Fill in the blanks.*

My biggest limitation is _ME_

Someone who has succeeded who also dealt with this

limitation is _TERRA_

One small step I can make towards my dreams is

JUST DO IT!

CHAPTER *Nine*

Possibility

I'm grateful for my brain. My noggin is creative and out of the box, which has created powerful opportunities for me. My mind has questionable tendencies, however, and can get trapped fixating on weird thoughts. *Why does that light fixture look like a boob? This mountain range makes me hungry for broccoli!* But I see what it's trying to do. *Most of the time.*

Now remember, your brain's primary job is to keep you safe[11] (*not all heroes wear capes, sometimes they just wear skin),* which means that if you get hurt or if an incident occurs that doesn't feel like rainbows and sunshine, your mind will bookmark that memory, encouraging you to hide under the table like a preschooler next time an experience feels similar. If you touch a hot stove, your brain remembers you burned yourself so it puts in a mental note that stoves equal pain. *Some of us need to touch the stove 15 times to get that memo.* Although emotional pain is perceptual, it does the same thing. Oh, you fell in love? Got hurt? Never opening up to feeling that again!

When there's a bad experience, our brain creates a cause and effect relationship with that memory. "If 'x' happens, then 'y' will happen, and I will feel 'z'." Hey, we can't be mad at our mind's protective features. Your brain is going above and beyond trying to make sure you don't ever feel that way again. *How thoughtful.* This feature, however, simultaneously blocks the possibility of you putting yourself out there and finding true love and happiness.

Part of our work is collaborating with our mind and includes brainstorming alternative outcomes. Remembering just because your result might end up poorly, doesn't mean it has to. *You still shouldn't touch a hot stove. There's a rather high risk of being a burn victim.* Creating possibility requires you to see all sides of the situation. If I take a risk and start a business, I give the business a chance to be supported and successful. If I open myself up to love, I could fall in love with someone incredible. Our brain desperately needs to know a positive outcome is possible. If you don't believe you can achieve what you set out for, you are less likely to reach it.

At one point in human history, we thought that running a four-minute mile was impossible. Rumor has it, people believed your heart would explode in your chest if you tried. Runners chased this record for decades but never shattered the four-minute barrier. Until this guy named Roger Bannister came in and was like, "Hold my beer," and on May 6, 1954, Dr. Bannister ran a mile in just under four minutes. *Like a boss.* Within 46 days, despite no one having broken the record previously, Bannister's record was surpassed by mere seconds by his rival, Landy. *Dick move, Landy, dick move.* To this day, more people have climbed Mount Everest than run a sub four-minute mile.[12]

Seeing possibility is necessary for moving through fear, pushing limitations, and thriving in tough situations. We have to believe that what we want is feasible.

Look to people who have surmounted a situation similar to yours. You can find famous spokesmodels all over for just about any topic. Need help getting over a break-up? Someone broke up with Jennifer Aniston. *Jaw drop.* Beyoncé had her heart crushed. *Get it together, Jay-Z.* One loser even ditched J-Lo and her perfect ass. If you need help overcoming addiction, Demi Lovato has had great success with sobriety and has even produced relatable songs like, "Warrior."

Most importantly, we have to believe, even amidst tragedy and chaos, something better is on its way. Did you know Walt Disney went bankrupt seven times before becoming a success? Oprah was told she would never make it in television. J.K. Rowling found herself rejected by a slew of publishers whilst living homeless prior to the success of *Harry Potter*. My point is, find a story, a role model, even a person in your life you admire, who has beaten the odds. Listen to what they did or went through and how they came out on the other side. Begin creating possibility by identifying examples. Anything is possible, exceptional outcomes are just as likely as lousy outcomes. It's about getting brave and challenging your brain to consider other options.

Try this. *Fill in the blanks.*

Look at a problem that you've been having or an area of life you are trying to overcome.

How are you viewing this problem and the possibilities?

_____

List other ways you might view the problem:

_____

Name someone you know that has gone through this or something similar and thrived (If you're not sure, do some research): ___DIAMOND AT 60___

OPEN my mouth so others can hear my voice

76

CHAPTER *Ten*

Fear

You know in the Disney Pixar movie *Inside Out* how there are several emotions that control us? Our big one is the purple people-eater known as fear. We are scared of our own shadow. We are afraid that people won't like us. We are petrified they will. *Maybe they will like us too much and suffocate us with their presence. Run!*

We are nervous that we won't succeed, but also freaked about what will happen if we do. We are terrified of commitment, but also afraid of abandonment. I mean, in what paradoxical world does all of this fear make any sense? Fear causes us to make ridiculously terrible choices. Apprehension makes us play small and "stay safe" even if what we are clinging to isn't actually safe.

Fear is like your overbearing mother, a helicopter parent of sorts. The one who pours antibacterial liquid on your hands every time you touch a railing. Fear hangs tight in the driver's seat forcing you to sit in the back while he drives all over the road in a frantic manner. There you are hanging out in the back holding onto those ceiling handles (*Were they made for moments like this? I mean, what are those handles really for anyway? Not just to hang dry cleaning?*), praying to God that you make it out alive. Fear makes you feel like you have not an ounce of control. When the reality is, you can tap fear on the shoulder and say, "Excuse me, I'm way better at driving than you are. Can you take a back seat please?" *You don't have to be a jerk to fear, you can be polite.*

At any given time, you can take your life back. You can decide what your perception is going to be and if you are going to filter everything through the lens of fear. Here's the thing; life can be scary. *I once woke up at 3 a.m. to a bat in my bedroom.* Life can also be seriously fantastic. Our world is a duality of rainbows and unicorns as well as tragedy and loss.   One of my favorite talks is Jim Carrey's commencement speech when he discusses how his father wanted to be a comedian. Jim explained his father thought it was safer to be an accountant until the day he got laid off and had to struggle to provide for his family. His final lines include, "You can fail at something you don't want, so you might as well take a chance on doing what you love."

Every single moment you make a choice. You decide if you are going to live inside of your fear or not. There will always be something to be afraid of, so you have to choose whether or not fear is serving you. That foreboding feeling can trick you into stupid choices and keep you grasping on to something that is clearly not working. Are you going to grasp on to your ex, who makes you feel insignificant and unimportant, in case you don't ever feel connected to anyone ever again? The one who probably is dating at least four other girls. *Dump his ass.* We keep really dumb things in our life— dumb thoughts, dumb beliefs, dumb people, and dumb jobs—out of fear of what will happen if we let them go.

Acknowledge your fear by labeling it. Say, "Hey fear, how are you trying to keep me safe?" Challenge your fear by posing the questions: What is on the other side of this fear? What rewards will come physically, mentally, or emotionally once I kick this apprehension's ass? Fear is a narrow focus. By asking better questions we can expand our focus and shift into action.

SO IMPORTANT

Fear is important. You know, so we don't, like, fall off a cliff while hiking. Become aware of your fear, even become friends with it. But don't you dare let your fear take over. Get curious about where your fears originated. Talk out loud about fear-based thoughts or write down and dissect them. Sometimes thoughts spin in our heads and when we say them out loud the fact that we even had the thought feels silly. Expand your brain and implement positive possibility. You have to know your own power. Fear, like everything else that is going on in our heads, is only a thought that you keep thinking.

When I was in the sixth grade, I had a birthday party where no one showed up. My twelfth birthday only included me, my sister, my best friend Kellie, and the boy across the street who my mom lured over with a slice of the best vanilla cake. I felt completely and utterly humiliated. After all, I was relatively popular at the time, I was certain my friends would come, but they didn't.

After the solo birthday, this overwhelming fear kicked in that no one would show up for me. From sixth grade on, I never referred to anything as a party. I would downplay any event I hosted. "Oh, you know, just a handful of people getting together" (even if I had invited 50). *No biggie.* Downplaying my parties wasn't a big deal. In fact, I learned there was a reward to it. Underselling these events made it better for me when a ton of people did show up. "Wow, Nichole, I thought you were only expecting a couple of people?" *I know. I know. They simply can't stay away.*

I learned to get a tight grip on my fear and disguise it in a rewarding way until my career began to take off about four years ago. I had started Clarity which was a successful coaching and therapeutic business. I received a slew of ideas which involved me putting myself out there in the community. *Gasp.* I had dreamed of creating my own motivational speaking event, similar to the popular TED talks, but with a focus on personal development and a hint of spiritual flair.

The event space was practically gifted to us by the owner. Smaller venues were going to charge triple what this venue was willing to charge. But here was my fear, guys, this venue held 500 people. 500! Which meant if a significant amount of people did NOT show up to my event, it would look completely empty. My fear kicked into overdrive as I tried to casually back out. At this point, my business partner and I had gained enough momentum, we simply couldn't. Our speakers were lined up. Our venue was set. We were amping up the social media advertisements and partaking in radio and news interviews. *Fuck. We were really going to do this.*

Meanwhile, back in the base of my skull, I was in panic mode. My motivational speaking event triggered memories of my twelfth birthday. No one was going to come except maybe my business partner's great aunt. I would have to find some sort of cover-up. I even preplanned. "Well, it was spring break and everyone was out of town. I could see why no one showed up." "The weather was supposed to be really bad, no one wanted to go out in the snow. I don't blame them!" Everything in me wanted to cancel this damn event to avoid facing the feeling of being let down or embarrassed. My business partner, Christy, refused to let me.

Lucky for me, Christy is a dreamer. "What if we sell out?" she said. "What if this event changes lives? What if it's a flop but we connect with people who will help make the event better next year?" Fear limits you to only one possibility and mine was failure in the form of humiliation. Listening to the other possibilities alleviated some of the fear surrounding the event.

In February of 2015, we hosted our first annual Clarity Connects Motivational Speaking Event. 150 people showed up. 150! Now, it's not 500, but this event contained more than just me, my sister, my friend Kellie, and neighborhood kids lured by baked goods. I was proud. We recently hosted our fourth Clarity Connects, nearly hitting capacity at 450 attendees. I am so grateful for the support of friends pushing me to follow through instead of allowing my fear to take over. Fear will ask you to play small and demand you shrink to fit its requirements, creating very real illusions. Your job is to push through the uncomfortable. Question everything. Find support and people willing to challenge you. Most importantly, take a deep breath and do it anyway.

Now I have to mention something because I would be doing us both a disservice if I didn't. After the second successful Clarity Connects, we did attempt to go on the road and host our event in a town three hours away. The venue was a gorgeous old church. We built a lineup of incredible speakers. But it bombed. *Totally effing bombed.* We canceled three weeks before the show due to only selling two tickets, both to Christy's aunt.

Although having to cancel sucked, it didn't activate that same fear or embarrassment. Instead, this failure helped highlight how taxing it is planning an event out of town. We realized our lack of desire to host the event elsewhere in the future. Our learning curve helped us improve our marketing and branding, as well as get clear on ways we could make our New York event the best one yet. When you push through a fear and it still doesn't work out, it doesn't mean you weren't meant to experience that outcome. Look for the lessons. What can you take from this experience?

Allow yourself to identify the fear. Know that moving through fear will be uncomfortable, but the possibility once you are on the other side can be so worthwhile. Making choices that align with potential rather than fear can launch you into a better job, a better relationship, and a better life. You are in the driver's seat.

Try this. *Fill in the blanks.*

What am I afraid of? IT BEING TOO MUCH? I WON'T BE WELL ENOUGH TO HANDLE IT

What am I worried will happen? I WORK HARD ; IT DOESN'T HAPPEN

What are other potential outcomes? IT DOES HAPPEN? I AM WELL

Try thanking the fear for how it's protecting you, then ask it to step aside.

CHAPTER *Eleven*

Gratitude

Stepping off the cruise ship into Belize, a third world country located in Central America, I felt this gloomy energy wash over me. The lush trees and scenic views weren't implying doom, yet the air felt uncertain. The group I was with hopped on the tour bus off to our excursion—cave tubing through the jungle! It was an exhausting trip to the center of the jungle, hours spent on a rickety, non-air-conditioned bus sounding like it could break down at any given moment.

I window-watched as the Belizean kids walked to school. Piping in over the speaker was our tour guide as he announced how in this particular area, kids can barely afford school supplies. The further away from the ship dock we were, the more we saw alarming scenes. Houses topped with branches and brush, in place of roofs. Children, no more than 10-years-old, standing on corners with machine guns. Houses built on stilts for safety during floods and protection against the intrusion of wild animals. One-room schoolhouses with gaping holes for windows.

The scenarios caught my eye more-so because they were issues I never experienced living in a middle-class community in upstate New York. I had windows on my house, a roof too. A New Kids on the Block comforter dressed the queen size bed in the middle of my very own bedroom. *A whole collection of Elvis dolls.* I had never seen a machine gun, let alone held one in my hands. I knew going into school was safe from lions and tigers and bears, (*oh my)* because my school had windows—many of them!

I remember this moment because it was the first time I felt extreme gratitude for my way of life. My sheltered self didn't realize destitution, like here in

Belize, existed. *This is embarrassing to admit.* I mean here I was on a cruise ship, traveling internationally at 16-years-old. As a white female, who had grown up in a predominantly white, middle-class community, my concerns were really nit-picky in comparison to what I witnessed in Belize.

A fast-track to changing your negative mindset starts with gratitude.[13] When our conscious or unconscious mind is fixated on the areas of suckery in our lives, gratitude flips our focus. A grateful life begins by us perceiving how lucky we are to have school supplies, a roof over our heads, or to even have woken up this morning because, well, there's plenty of people who didn't.

I remember recently learning about a program that donated feminine products to third-world countries because young girls missed school for a whole week due to not having access to tampons.[14] Now, I don't know about you but before reading that article, I'd never felt overly grateful while putting in a tampon. Taking everyday luxuries for granted is common. We begin to expect life to be a certain way.

Can you imagine living as if every little thing is a gift? You wake up in the morning stoked to have even opened your eyes! Also, how cool that you HAVE eyes and eyesight? You put your hand on your heart—holy shit! It's beating. All. By. Itself! You don't even have to think about your heart functioning, it just beats! That's bananas. You flick on the lights, and wow, you have electricity! How amazing is it that someone created electricity? I mean, you just flip a switch and let there be light! Next, you hop in your luxurious nice, warm shower and feel in awe—you get both warm and clean water! And breakfast. Oh, man, the universe is outdoing itself at this point because there is food in your house. Yummy, scrumptious food that nourishes your body! How great is this morning?! You look around to share your excitement and you might notice your spouse, your kids, your pets. What a damn miracle, you get to share this with another one of God's creatures. This day is out of control. Then you go outside getting in your…wait for it…CAR! You have a car that runs! A vehicle that takes you from point A to point B, almost every single time! To your JOB, none the less. You have a job. Oh. Em. Gee. Amazing! They pay you to be there. Can you believe your luck?! Maybe your employer occasionally even pays you to take a vacation—what on earth? Is this real life? This life is so epic. There's gifts around every corner.

You get my point, right? Being alive is a total miracle. There are people who would do anything to have your life. Even if you look at my ramblings and think, yeah but I don't have a job or car or a whatever. I'll say to you, but you woke up this morning, right? You have your limbs? Your hearing? Your eyesight, perhaps? Your lungs are working on their own? Any of the above? It's a great day! Find something to be grateful for, even if you have to dig a little for it.

I like to use the word *love* instead of gratitude. I connect with the word better. Considering word choice when you think of gratitude can help you deepen the statement and feel into it rather than simply muttering the sentence while you get ready. The connection to your feelings will begin to positively reprogram your brain and neural pathways, creating more awareness of positive situations and perceptions. I say phrases like, "I love when the sky is bright blue and the sun is shining." "Holy crap, I just adore the night sky." "I love when the kids wake up and get ready on time. Man, that makes the morning easier." Some people use "thankful" or "happy." Connecting with your own gratitude is an individual and personal experience. Play around and see what feels best for you.

I know how hard gratitude can be when life has clearly been loading you up with lemons, when you don't even like lemons. *I always say when life hands you lemons, make a lemon-drop martini!* I need to tell you a story about someone who inspired the hell out of me with turning lemons into a life well lived.

Have you heard of the late Jim MacLaren? This badass was a powerhouse athlete in college, playing both lacrosse and football. When he was 22, MacLaren was in a motorcycle accident and lost his left leg below the knee. Losing a limb should be a free pass to give up, right? But, Jim didn't raise his white flag. Instead, he went on to do an Ironman competition and ran a marathon in 3 hours and 16 minutes. *If you are not a runner, anything under four hours is ridiculous, let alone with one leg.*

Now, I know what you are thinking—that's super inspiring. Here's this man with challenges thrown at him and he's slaying these blocks left and right, good stuff, Nichole, good stuff. *But wait, there's more.* Eight years later after his initial accident when he lost his leg, MacLaren was racing in a triathlon. He was on the bike-riding portion of the race when a van turned into the blocked off course striking him. Jim was left a quadriplegic. God gifted Jim a double free pass to quit, I mean the man could no longer use his legs or arms. But did he call it a day? No, Jim MacLaren spent the remainder of his life inspiring the masses as a motivational speaker and author.

I found Jim's story to be life-altering. Let it act as a reminder to not fall victim to your circumstances. Take whatever power you have left and run with it. Allow Jim's life to act as a prompt of gratitude for whatever you have, even if it seems like you've been beaten down over and over again. Find something to be grateful for. The smallest thing. The sky. The stars at night. The potential. The experience. It's all important and relevant to your journey.

Try this.

For the next 60 days write down ten NEW things to be grateful for each day. Do not repeat any. This will help you seek out positive things that make you happy in your world.

CHAPTER *Twelve*

Subconscious

After I had my second daughter, I decided the time to stop eating mass quantities of chocolate for two had finally arrived. Baby didn't need the chocolate cheesecake anymore because she was outside of my body drinking milk like a champ. My body, however, still craved an entire ice cream cake for dinner.

I pushed through for three whole days with an unscathed nutrient-filled, sugarless diet. When on a blistering cold day in late February, a month when all bad things happen, an evil seven-year-old Girl Scout did a cute little tap, tap, tap on my door. In her hands, the Thin Mints I'd ordered a few months ago. I placed the cookies on the counter and pulled up a chair. I was just going to stare. I wasn't going to eat them. *Deep breaths.* The longer I stared, I realized they were staring back.

These cookies wanted me to just smell them. I did the right thing to do in that very moment—I cracked them open and breathed the chocolate-minty magnificence up into my nostrils. *If I've ever considered snorting anything, this was that moment.* I had one solid hour of willpower before not just consuming one or two cookies but vigorously shoving the entire box down my throat. *Warning: Never look at the calories on Girl Scout cookies. Specifically, following consumption of the entire box.*

I really did want to make changes, I swear. But faced with my arch nemesis, the familiarity of my sugar addiction capsized my willpower, and my desire to shed baby weight was catapulted out the window.

Remember how we chatted earlier about your brain being a stupid, yet effective machine? Our brain-machine is built to be *cybernetic*, which means that it's built as a system to self-regulate—like a thermostat.

Let's pretend that we are in the dead of winter. *I live in Upstate NY. It's winter a lot.* You've set your thermostat at a comfortable 70 degrees. Your doorbell

rings and some ass-wipe approaches to sell you a

vacuum. Out of politeness, you let him talk for a few

minutes, but you're certainly not inviting him in, giving

him the impression you are interested. Here you are

standing in the doorway with the cold winter breeze

blasting into your toasty warm home. After there is a

clear victor in the vacuum standoff, you notice the whole

front foyer is ice cold. Here's where your thermostat

rushes to the rescue. "I've got it. I will get you guys back

up to 70 in no time," your thermostat shouts, blasting hot

air for a half hour until you safely return to a

comfortable 70 degrees.

Self-regulation works well for thermostats. Not

nearly as awesome for people who desire to make a

change. Up until we are about seven-years-old our brain

is so formable. Our mind is designed to absorb

information creating subconscious systems, thought

patterns, and mental loops, helping us live safely. After a

while your brain runs on autopilot and before you know

it you're thinking, feeling, and acting in ways that are a reflection of your subconscious patterns. So, what I'm trying to say is your subconscious is annoying and rigid. And I get it, these loops have been looping a long time.

Our conscious mind and our subconscious mind are two totally separate entities functioning together. Our conscious mind wants to improve. Make better choices. The part that decides to go back to school, lose weight, or leave a toxic relationship. The conscious mind is responsible for your *why* and your long-term goals, which is the reason your *why* is so important—it helps you stay on top of your willpower. Willpower helps the subconscious stay in check or create lasting change.

The subconscious, on the other hand, is the blocker. Your subconscious looks out for you by making everything the exact same as it has always been. It whispers sweet nothings in your ear like, "You love that cake, remember? Just one bite and everything will be back to normal." Your subconscious is predictable, begging for the same route to work every day. Deviating

from the same routes feels uncomfortable, trying to sabotage you until you go back to "normal."

This is why making changes and expanding possibilities is challenging. Our conscious brain can only do so much. Our conscious brain can say, "Oh hey, I'm ready to lose a little weight," and our subconscious brain will play along until 2 p.m. or even two weeks later while spying chocolate cake in the break room, looking extra moist and delicious. Our subconscious is savage and built to protect our thought patterns and behavioral patterns, even when they aren't serving us.

True change is incredibly reliant on changing the subconscious mind. Creating awareness of how your subconscious functions is the first step to changing it. Remember you can't get the deodorant stain off your little black dress if you don't realize it's there. We can even acknowledge its urges, cravings, or desires aloud. Saying, "I want to drunk dial my ex even though he treated me poorly is an urge from the part of my brain wanting familiarity." Labeling the urge to retreat back to what's familiar, helps to detach the energy of the desire and gives your conscious brain an opportunity to step in and make an active decision.

Secondly, we want to think about how responsive our brain is to repetition. Repeating information is how you develop deep-seated patterns and any repetition of a thought or action alters your brain.[15] *For better or worse.* Developing new mantras, intentions, affirmations and saying them out loud, in your head, or writing them down over and over helps. Hypnotic suggestion is known to create huge shifts in your subconscious.[16] In the next few chapters, we will talk about the role of spontaneity in shifting your subconscious as well as how self-care can change the looping of your unconscious mind.

Try this. *Fill in the blanks.*

List your biggest obstacle: _____

Re-connect with your "why" statement. For the next two hours, create awareness of how you speak to yourself about this topic. Keep tabs of automatic thoughts or urges around it. Take a deep breath into the thought. Write down what it is you truly want for yourself and your life, in regards to this obstacle.

I WANT TO MAKE AN IMPACT IN OTHERS LIVES.

Repeat tonight.

CHAPTER *Thirteen*

Spontaneity

Routine is important. Every day when we commit to bettering ourselves or learning a new skill, we grow a little. Every exercise we do, we build momentum to achieving a healthier, happier body. Every time we meditate we add to our brain's expansion and ease. And let's face it, progress, even at an inch-by-inch level, equates with happiness. The problem is, when everything looks exactly the same, making changes is hard. *Especially if our routine isn't focused on self-improvement and includes Netflix and glazed donuts.*

When we wake up to the same chaos of shoving breakfast down our kids' throats and hurrying them out the door, when we do the same routine of walking our dog and heading to bed at 10 p.m., our brain gets comfortable. *Why change if I can pull out a blanket throw and nap?* The problem with routines is if nothing changes, nothing changes.

Did you know despite thinking around 60,000 thoughts per day, the majority (estimated at around 90%) were the same thoughts we produced yesterday, according to research done by Fred Luskin of Stanford University?[17] *That's pretty effing boring.*

We become who we believe ourselves to be and our external environments are a direct reflection. Our belief in who we are is vital to the creation of our life circumstances. Have you ever met someone who is a self-proclaimed bitch? And when you hang out you think to yourself, "Wow, they really are a bitch." You might notice interactions are often conflictual or defensive. We act and think in ways that reinforce who we believe ourselves to be. If you are dying to make a change you have to do some restructuring of your self-proclamations. You can change who you believe you are, by switching up your day-to-day routine.

Enter a booty-shaking competition in the Bahamas because, homie, we are about to get spontaneous! *Possibly based on a true story.* Spontaneity is a necessity when making big changes, shaking up subconscious programming. When we give ourselves permission to be different, acting and thinking in alternative ways becomes a piece of cake.

Shifting and changing is easiest in a different environment. Consider the anxious person who goes away on a meditation retreat and comes back totally Zen. New settings, fresh activities, and different people allow hidden or forgotten parts of ourselves to emerge, giving us freedom. *No one knows me here and expects me to be a certain way. I can sing karaoke. I can ride a mechanical bull. I can drink twelve shots of Mexican tequila and dance in the streets with a police officer.* Spontaneity also taps directly into our highest selves. We are most "us" when we aren't trying so hard and follow our impulses. Our authentic selves chase desires without second guessing if we will look stupid doing it.

Making split-second decisions, letting our intuition guide us to that belly dancing class, or drifting to a faraway town, gives us direct access to our highest selves.

Flow is found in spontaneity. Perhaps it gives you permission to not be so serious or to release control. Embracing this quality gives you the ability to accept and work with whatever shows up in your world, improving your ability to manage stress. There are so many ways to practice spontaneity. Let's explore.

Mix up your routine

Use a new recipe. Go test drive a new car. Walk through homes for sale. Fold clothes upstairs instead of downstairs. Wake up earlier. Go to bed later. Shake up your damn life. You can find new things to try by listening to your intuition. Where is your soul guiding you? What activities do you have a natural curiosity about? If you drink wine on Wednesdays, try a whiskey on Friday instead. If you watch TV after work, try a book instead. Take note of your routines and play with switching them around, including new activities, or removing activities no longer serving you.

Say yes

If you find yourself saying no to opportunities, try saying yes. Go bowling with your co-workers. Attend the mixer solo. If you say yes too often, switch it around and say no.

Be silly

I worked in a pre-k classroom and found myself amused with how kids behave. *If Suzie wants to sing "Old McDonald Had a Farm" in the middle of circle time, she sure as heck will.* Kids know exactly what they want and have fun in the process. Children turn anything into a game, including grocery shopping or tying shoelaces. Giving yourself permission to enjoy life, be childlike, will loosen up rigid thought patterns. Dance around, sing at the top of your lungs, paint terrible pictures, and rediscover play.

Gift yourself a get-away

There's power in new places and energy in new cities. For us small towners, traveling is a reminder life exists beyond our normal environment. Small-town living is restricting when you leave to get bread and milk and spend an extra hour at the store because you ran into your childhood best friend's mom, six different clients, and the guy who works at the gym's front desk. *Hey Tim!* Being temporarily unknown is a superpower, helping you decide which parts of yourself are worth keeping and exploring personality traits you're ready to upgrade. Along with new places, you'll experience new experiences—the idea behind "when in Rome." The more you challenge your brain's expansion with new ventures and settings, the better your brain will function. As we know, possibilities are essential to creating change in your mindset.

While writing this book, I went to a cabin in Vermont to be alone. The cabin was quaint but had no running water. The bathroom and shower were outside. I've never showered outside. *Have you showered outside?* After two days of avoiding this outdoor shower, I finally caved to my own stench and in 50-degree weather took my first steaming hot outdoor shower! Being naked outside is magical. You would think an outdoor shower wouldn't be a huge deal but the feeling of freedom bled into a series of decisions leading to a solo hike in the Adirondack mountains on the way home. If you can't travel to Vermont, consider the power of going for a walk in a different neighborhood or even the next town over.

Pick up a new hobby

A year or two ago, I took a series of boxing classes. I have to be honest, I felt like a total badass. *Watch out, Rocky!* I love boxing. I effortlessly unleashed years of suppressed anger onto the heavy bag. However, the time came where we began sparring, meaning my instructor asked me to punch another living, breathing person. I was so out of my element. I preach peace and all things sparkly, I can't hit you in the face. *Sorry, not sorry!* But my lovely instructor, two-time world heavyweight champion, Bonnie Mann, forced me out of my comfort zone. I took a deep breath and punched Bonnie— repeatedly for 30-seconds straight. Sparring led to a brief high followed by a genuine urge to vomit. *Hitting people isn't nearly as fun as it sounds. I'll stick to the heavy bag.* However, realizing I could get out of my comfort zone gave me the confidence to make changes in other areas of my life. With a new hobby you also have the chance to make friends and focus all of your energy into the present moment. *Mostly because you have no idea what you are doing.* Channeling energy into the now, eliminates worry and depression by realizing in this very moment, you're totally okay.

Get uncomfortable

In 2014, I ran an eleven-mile mud run called the Tough

Mudder, a race designed by the military. The course is

rigorous, challenging, and requires upper body strength I

do not possess. A few of the obstacles, for full effect,

include electrocution, jumping off a high platform, and

swimming through a long dumpster of ice water. This, to

date, is one of the hardest races I've ever run.

You would think electrocution would seal the

deal on the worst obstacle, but for me, it was the 15-foot

platform. I'm not afraid of heights, per se, but I'm

terrified of the feeling of falling. My best bet was to get

right up there without thinking and just jump. As I

approached the deck, I stood waiting for the runners

before me to swim out of the way. The pause gave me

time to formally assess why the hell I would be jumping

off a super-high platform, already covered head to toe in

mud, cuts, and bruises. *It's borderline insane.* But, I did

it! When you push past your fear to accomplish

something you thought you couldn't do, your confidence

ramps up. The memory helps push other perceived

limits, reminding your brain of the time you were

uncomfortable but successfully did something anyway.

Visualize

Our brains have no idea what is real and what is our

imagination, meaning you can create change simply by

visualizing or pretending. You can even subtly trick your

brain by including music or items from a time when you

were at your best. In 1979, Ellen Langer invited two

groups of men to a monastery in New Hampshire. One

group was asked to reminisce about their younger years.

The other men were transported to a 1959 time-capsule.

Everything down to the clothing and newspapers was

reflective of a younger time period. Although Langer

never found funding to publish her article, she reflected

that after the stay, the men who were transported to the

time-capsule looked younger, tested higher on

intelligence exams, and even those who came in weak

were running around the front lawn playing touch

football.[18] With both visualizing and connecting with music, items, or people who inspire a younger or different way of thinking, changes can occur.

If your resources are limited, just envision yourself doing one of these activities. Your brain does not know what is real or perceived which is why we can have a total panic attack with only a perceived threat. Visualizing also creates a memory of an experience even if it hasn't happened, which is why envisioning who you want to become is so powerful.[19]

Try this. *Fill in the blanks.*

If we were to upgrade your life, who would you become?

VACATION JULIE

What would you do, think, or say as this upgraded version?

RELAXED, FUNNER, TIME TO BE MORE POLISHED

Where would you love to go? Somewhere close by? Far away? FLORIDA IS GOOD

What have you always wanted to try or learn?

YOGA RETREAT, BOXING

Write it down. Create a plan of action.

LOOK INTO REFUEL WITH THAT GENTLE MAN

CHAPTER *Fourteen*

Self-Care

Justin Bieber had a valid point when he said, "You should go and love yourself." *I'm absolutely positive he was talking about self-care.* If we begin to think of the brain and body as machines, we can recognize you must put high-quality oil in the engine to keep them running. Updating the database will make a machine run smoother. Taking extra care will ensure it lasts longer. Too long without checking on ourselves can negatively impact us mentally, emotionally, and spiritually. There are a few basic activities we can do to keep our brains top-notch.

 Meditate

As it turns out, mediation isn't just for woo-woo spiritualists. *I can say this because I'm a woo-woo*

spiritualist. Meditating is better than cupcakes and prescription medication. From reducing stress, improving concentration, and increasing happiness by decreasing activity on the "negative" side of the brain, meditation is where it's at.[20] Meditation is one of the best ways to tap into your own willpower, improving your control over your subconscious patterns. According to Kelly McGonigal's book *The Willpower Instinct*, as little as three total hours of meditating has been shown to positively change the gray matter of the brain, increasing focus and emotional stability. Word on the street, meditating for 15-20 minutes per day even acts as a low dose anti-depressant AND slows the aging process.[21] *Pencil me in for four hours. I'm 30 now.*

When I first started meditating I didn't know what the hell I was doing. *So, you cross your legs, just so. Your fingertips are supposed to be doing something, touching maybe?* I was so worked up about meditating wrong, I couldn't relax. *Which is sort of the point.*

Let me demystify this whole process for you. Meditating is simply the act of bringing your energy and focus to the now moment. That's it. Some people do active meditation while they run, clean, play an instrument, or have sex. Active meditation is any activity you lose time while doing. Although there are plenty of different techniques proven effective, let me make it easy for you.

⅄ If you are new to meditation, go slow. Sit, stand, or lie down however you feel comfortable. Your eyes can be open or shut. Now take a slow deep breath in, focusing on the air flowing down through your lungs and back out. *Boom! You just meditated.* Meditation can be as simple as focused breathing. Different ways to do focused breathing include counting to four as you inhale, counting out six as you exhale. *Or any number that feels good to you.* Inhaling a color and exhaling a different color is another fun technique. Visualization of any kind, including guided visualizations found on YouTube, are powerful. You could even repeat an intention or mantra while you breathe. I encourage those ready to pop their meditation cherry to start small. Try focused breathing for 30 seconds. Any thoughts that pop into your head, just say, "hello" to them and return your attention to your breathing. *It's totally normal.* If 30 seconds feels easy, move to two minutes. You can continue expanding the amount of time you meditate. Your best results will happen with 20 or more minutes of meditation per day.

☆ Movement

Everyone on the planet is advising you to work out. If your social media isn't popping with Beach Body coaches selling you their newest workout, you can trade with me. *No disrespect to the side hustle and all the positivity that Beach Body is putting out into the world.* Movement—whether you are training for a marathon or stretching prior to getting out of bed in the morning—is vital for your mental health.

Research suggests that exercise improves memory, thinking, focus, and problem-solving skills, as well as prevents anxiety and depression.[22] *Not too shabby.* A study at the University of Texas Southwestern Medical Center even created clinical guidelines for recommended exercise "dosage" that would have similar effects as antidepressants.[23]

I love to run but I've become a huge yoga fan, after years of finding the practice "too slow and boring." Yoga is great for any skill level and teaches breathing alongside movements. Help yourself out as you are working to change your mind, by including regular movement in your day. Even if you take an extra-long stretch before getting out of bed or throw a dance party while making breakfast in the morning, you're doing it. *Every morning should start with a dance party!*

Although I'm emphasizing movement, I'll encourage you to consider that movement is just one part of physical self-care. Getting a good night's sleep, having healthy sexual interactions, drinking enough water, and fueling your body with clean foods and fewer

YOU ARE WORTHY OF LIVING A LIFE YOU ARE PASSIONATE ABOUT!

cupcakes are all important to maintaining and improving

healthy cognitive functioning.

Self-love

Re-wiring your old mental loops and exchanging ways

of thinking for upgraded models can be difficult. In the

beginning, changing your mind is honestly annoying.

Who wants to monitor everything their mind is doing?

While in the phase of shifting your thoughts, be

intentionally compassionate with yourself. Forgive the

days when you didn't nail it. Greet yourself with love

and kindness on challenging days. Hold space for

difficult emotions and honor their purpose on your

journey. Use the activities and the ideas in this book, to

improve your self-perception, including awareness of

how you are speaking to yourself, being intentional

about how you want to feel, and expanding possibilities.

You are worthy of love and belonging. You are worthy

of feeling fantastic in your own skin. You are worthy of

living a life you are passionate about.

Take good care of yourself. Be kind to yourself. Treat yourself in the ways that you'd want your children or anyone you love, to cherish, respect, and love themselves. Speak kindly. Act kindly. Just these acts alone can shift everything.

CHAPTER *Fifteen*

How to Change Your Mind

Now you might be saying, "I see the concepts. Thoughts are powerful and I need to be better about noticing the rough ones. But changing your thoughts around is a lot of work." Yes, it is. I won't bullshit you; reworking your brain is a total pain in the ass because of the way your brain is built. But I promise you, it's possible and rewarding! This is the part where you all get mad at the realization that you could've simply skipped the explanation of each chapter and shortcut to this one. Everything you need to know is right here. I'm going to walk you through everything we just talked about to help you create lasting changes in your mindset that will bleed into your self-image, your happiness, your relationships, your career, and even your decisions.

You can use these concepts to form a routine. Start with one area that you think may benefit you most. I always think, "If I had _____, I'd feel better and be more productive." Find what you're needing most to start making changes. Perhaps you need more energy and feel most energized when you start your day with a workout or when you are drinking more water. Perhaps you just need more sleep and feel meditation would help. Maybe you're most concerned about your thoughts and how negative they are so you'd like to be more aware and start a meditation practice, gratitude practice, or intention-writing practice. Start small and build on it. Give yourself a chance to succeed, get comfortable in that success, and build from there. Whatever it is, you've got this.

Why?

Decide *why* it's worth making changes. What will improve? What will it feel like? Create a *why*. Write it down. Revisit your *why* when obstacles approach.

Excuses

Find an example of someone who had similar circumstances who has followed their dreams. Identify the excuses you've created and see what you're really afraid of.

Perception

Get to know your view of the world, yourself, relationships, money, etc. and make sure the established views are helpful to you. If not, begin to decide what alternative thoughts might be believable and work towards changing your mind. If you can't postulate finding your soulmate, at least consider that you might find someone you don't hate to be around. Small mental moves make huge shifts.

Thoughts

Begin to create awareness of your thinking patterns and how it makes you feel. Are your thoughts disempowering you? What thoughts would feel better?

Even recognizing a thought and saying, "stop" or "cancel, clear, delete" can stop the momentum of negative energy in its tracks.

Intention

Decide what you want in each day, moment, and situation. Create a statement that reflects it. Your brain will begin to look for the truth of your intention in your external environment. Remember, an intention is a thought you have to be willing to believe. If you can't believe it, find a compromise then work your way up to a bigger belief. Set intentions for how you want to feel, for your self-perception, how you want a situation to go, for relationships, and for future goals. You can set an intention about anything. Repetition is the key to success. The more consistent and repetitive your intentions, the deeper and easier a new neural pathway is created. Remember, a belief is only a thought that we keep thinking. Make sure the thought is a good one!

Word choice

Your words have power. Pick and choose wisely.

Choose words with less power to decrease the emotional

intensity of challenging situations. Increase your self-

perception and self-esteem by using powerful words.

And occasionally swear.

Focus

Energy flows where focus goes. You have the power at

any given moment to shift your focus to a better thought,

better situation, or a different area of your life. Choosing

good questions shifts your focus. Instead of, "Why does

this always happen to me?", forcing your brain to

respond, "You're just not good enough", try asking a

question like, "What can I learn from this situation to

help me in my future?" or "What are my own strengths

and successes?" Shifting your focus can impact your

personal joy. You have access to any state of mind at

any time simply by rerouting your focus.

Limits

Limits do not exist. Limits are imposed not just by you
and your own fears, but by people who love you.
Identify the fear, take a deep breath, and push through.
No one can decide your limits but you! Rewards lie on
the other side of perceived restrictions.

Possibility

You have to believe what you want is possible.
Otherwise, your brain stops looking for proof inside
your head and in your external world. Find examples of
people who have overcome things to help drive you
towards your goals.

Fear

Fear is an illusion. Making changes can feel
uncomfortable but when we recognize how fear forces
us to settle and that a better life is on the other side, we
become willing to push through. Choose to have faith
your goals are achievable. Find a badass support system

for encouragement when you start to freak out. Trust the universe will show up for you.

Gratitude

Every single moment of every single day there is something to be thankful for. Search for what you love in this world. Develop a gratitude practice to help your brain refocus on the good stuff, creating positive neural pathways. A gratitude practice is scientifically proven to bring more joy,[24] helping your awareness of positive occurrences throughout the day.

Subconscious

Understand that you're not just failing when you set goals and then self-sabotage. Your brain is self-regulating. Knowing this information helps you recognize where you are getting stuck so you can employ some of the other tricks to override it, like spontaneity, meditation, and using your "why."

Spontaneity

Shake up your routine. Pick up a new hobby. Try something new, visit a new place, and give yourself permission to be a different version of yourself. *When in Rome.* Get out of your comfort zone and push your limits to build internal confidence which will spill over into other areas of your life.

Self-care

Take care of you. Your body and brain are machines needing good food, hydration, and a lot of love. Hold compassion for your process while working towards creating change. Speak to yourself with kindness and love.

CHAPTER *Sixteen*

Final Thoughts

You finished what you started! That's the first step to changing your life. Now it's up to you to begin creating awareness and shifts in your thinking. Try one practice at a time, get the hang of it, then add another technique when you feel ready. You are a work in progress, which is beautiful. We all are.

I hope this book has made you think about what goes on in your head. Question everything. *Always question everything.* You have so much power. You're practically a power ranger. Or Wonder Woman. Or a Care Bear fully equipped with a Care Bear stare. Or even Dorothy from the Wizard of Oz, because you've always had the power, my dear, you just had to see it for yourself.

It's time for me to release you back into the wild. But this time, you have everything you need to not just survive but thrive. I know you can live a life you love. Make the choice. Wishing you light, love, and clarity.

xo
Nichole Eaton

Resources

Below is a list of some of the books, research studies, and ideas or influencers I studied or drew from in the process of creating this book.

Books

Sincero, J. (2013). *You Are a Badass: How to Stop Doubting Your Greatness and Start Living an Awesome Life*

Grout, P. (2013). *E-Squared: Nine Do-It-Yourself Energy Experiments That Prove Your Thoughts Create Your Reality*

McGonigal, K. (2011). *The Willpower Instinct: How Self-Control Works, Why It Matters, and What You Can Do to Get More of It*

Influencers

Joe Dispenza, author and scientist, was featured in the film *What the BLEEP Do We Know?* Joe's work has a strong focus on understanding the brain and understanding the neurological process of changing your mind.

Tony Robbins is an author, entrepreneur, and life coach hosting self-help seminars all over the world. Robbins focuses on the power of the mind, changing your internal state, and reconnecting with your personal power.

Ideas

Cognitive Psychology:

Although there are many psychologists to credit in the development of Cognitive Psychology, Ulric Neisser is considered the "father" of the movement, interweaving research to gain a better understanding of internal

processing, patterns, attention, and problem-solving.

Cognitive Dissonance:

Psychologist Leon Festinger proposed the theory of

Cognitive Dissonance in his book *Theory of Cognitive*

Dissonance, in an attempt to explain how people reach

internal consistency.

Positive Psychology:

Martin Seligman coined the term Positive Psychology in

reference to the idea that we do not need to simply treat

mental illness, but preventatively foster positive mental

health to get the utmost value out of life.

Acknowledgments

I could've never finished this book without the insane amount of people who believed in me. Brandon, thank you for allowing me space, time, and solo vacays so I could write in peace and for believing in me on the days I didn't believe in myself. I love you. Samantha, my ride or die, thank you for reminding me of what I am here for through doubts, meltdowns, and 7 a.m. panicked phone calls. Nicole, thank you for reading everything I sent and for always expecting more out of me. Thank you for your emotional and mental support. Michelle, Liz, and Christy, thank you for supporting me along this path. For the countless clients who have asked over and over when my book will be done, believing in me and supporting me while I grow my business, my unwavering gratitude for your patience and love. I love you all.

About the Author

Nichole Eaton is an author, speaker, Lifestyle

Personality for the Future Life App, Creator of

Motivational Speaking event Clarity Connects, and Co-

Owner of Clarity, a progressive therapeutic company.

Nichole has brought dynamic transformation to hundreds

of clients with her unique style that interweaves her

experience as both a Licensed Mental Health Counselor

and an Intuitive. Nichole has a true passion for helping

others find their purpose, break through blocks, and

bring back their inner sparkle. When she's not busy

lighting up the world, you can find her baking up a storm

and playing on the playground with her two little girls.

Keep Up with Nichole

Instagram

NicholeEaton.Clarity

#RockYourSoul

Facebook

www.facebook.com/theclaritygirls

**Join the Rock Your Soul Community and connect
with like-minded friends:**

www.facebook.com/groups/rockyoursoulclarity

YouTube

www.youtube.com/claritygirls

Learn more or book a service with Nichole at

www.discoveryourawakening.com

Endnotes

[1] Kruglanski, A.W. (1989). The psychology of being "right": The problem with accuracy in social perception and cognition. *Psychological Bulletin.* 106(3):395-409

[2] Simon Sinek is a leader in the "Finding Your Why" movement to help people connect with their own why. You can learn more about this movement and connect with different "why" resources at www.startwithwhy.com

[3] McCrae, J. (2015). *The Scientific Reason Your Perception Creates Your Reality.* Retrieved from https://themindunleashed.com/2015/01/scientific-reason-perception-creates-reality.html

[4] Grout, P. (2013). *E-Squared: Nine Do-It-Yourself Energy Experiments That Prove Your Thoughts Create Your Reality*

[5] Kiger, P.J. (2018). *You Are Hardwired to Survive: How Your Brain Has Evolved to Be the Ultimate Survivor.* Retrieved from http://channel.nationalgeographic.com/brain-games/articles/you-are-hardwired-to-survive/

[6] Cognitive Psychology: Although there are many psychologists to credit in the development of Cognitive Psychology, Ulric Neisser is considered the "father" of the movement, interweaving research to gain a better understanding of internal processing, patterns, attention, and problem-solving.

[7] Festinger, F. (1962). *A Theory of Cognitive Dissonance.*

[8] Chung, C. & Pennebaker, J. (2007). The Psychological Functions of Function Words. In K. Fiedler (Ed.), *Frontiers of social psychology. Social communication* (pp. 343-359).

[9] Gallagher, W. (2009). *Rapt: Attention and the Focused Life*

[10] Chellingsworth, M., Farrand, P., & Rayson, K. (2013). Dealing with Worry in Low Intensity CBT. *The University of Exeter & Clinical Education Development and Research.*

[11] Kiger, P.J. (2018). *You Are Hardwired to Survive: How Your Brain Has Evolved to Be the Ultimate Survivor.* Retrieved from http://channel.nationalgeographic.com/brain-games/articles/you-are-hardwired-to-survive/

[12] Lehourites, C. (2018). *Roger Bannister, first to run sub 4-minute mile, dies at 88.* Retrieved from https://www.apnews.com/d6962d95359245f8a27a406af 57d534e

[13] Emmons, R.A. & McCullough, M.E. (2003). Counting blessings versus burdens: An experimental investigation of gratitude and subjective well-being in daily life. *Journal of Personality and Social Psychology. 84, 377-389*

[14] Lusk-Stover, O. (2016). *Globally, periods are causing girls to be absent from school.* Retrieved from

http://blogs.worldbank.org/education/globally-periods-are-causing-girls-be-absent-school

[15] Segerstrom, S. (2011). The structure and consequences of repetitive thought: How what's on your mind, and how, and how much, affects your health. *Psychological Science Agenda. American Psychological Association.*

[16] Mitchell, G. P. & Lundy, R. M. (1986). The effects of relaxation and imagery inductions on responses to suggestions. *International Journal of Clinical and Experimental Hypnosis, 34, 98-109.*

[17] Comaford, C. (2012) *Got Inner Peace? 5 Ways to Get it NOW.* Retrieved from https://www.forbes.com/sites/christinecomaford/2012/04/04/got-inner-peace-5-ways-to-get-it-now/#56f9197c6672

[18] Grierson, B. (2014). *What if Age Is Nothing but a Mind-Set?* Retrieved from https://www.nytimes.com/2014/10/26/magazine/what-if-age-is-nothing-but-a-mind-set.html

[19] Ranganathan, VK, Siemionow, V., Liu, JZ, Sahgal V., Yue, GH. (2014). From mental power to muscle power—gaining strength by using the mind. *Neuropsychologia. 42(7):944-56.*

[20] Shapiro, S.L., Schwartz, G. & Santerre, C. (2002). Meditation and Positive Psychology. *Handbook of Positive Psychology. 632-645*

[21] Quinn, C., King, B., Zanesco, A., Pokorny, J., Hamidi,

A., Jue, L., Epel, E., Blackburn, E. & Saron, C. (2015). Telomere lengthening after three weeks of intensive insight meditation retreat. *Psychoneuroendocrinology.61:26-27*

[22] Godman, H. (2014). *Regular exercise changes the brain to improve memory, thinking skills.* Retrieved from https://www.health.harvard.edu/blog/regular-exercise-changes-brain-improve-memory-thinking-skills-201404097110

[23] Dunn, A.L., Trivedi, M.H., Kampert, J.B., Clark, C.G. & Chambliss, H.O. (2005). Exercise treatment for depression: Efficacy and dose response. *American Journal of Preventive Medicine.*

[24] Emmons, R.A. & McCullough, M.E. (2003). Counting blessings versus burdens: An experimental investigation of gratitude and subjective well-being in daily life. *Journal of Personality and Social Psychology. 84, 377-389*

#RockYourSoul

I LOVE YOU : YOU ARE IMPORTANT
IN MY LIFE

I VALUE : APPRECIATE YOUR CONTINUED
LOVE : SUPPORT

AND I WANT TO SEE YOU LIVE A
WELL : PROSPEROUS LIFE.

INFO HAS COME TO ME THAT IS
IMPORTANT TO SHARE & WILL
IMPACT EVERY ONE'S LIFE IF YOU
ARE WILLING TO TAKE A LOOK.
WATCH STINK! AND TAKE
THE 3 CABINET CHALLENGE
YOU CAN EAT THE HEALTHIEST
FOOD, EXERCISE BUT IF THE
PERSONAL CARE : CLEANING PRODUCTS
YOU USE ARE

Made in the USA
Columbia, SC
02 November 2018